Original title:
A Roof Over My Head

Copyright © 2025 Creative Arts Management OÜ
All rights reserved.

Author: Clara Whitfield
ISBN HARDBACK: 978-1-80587-024-1
ISBN PAPERBACK: 978-1-80587-494-2

Homebound Horizons

In a cozy nook, my shoes are lost,
Couch diversions, what's the cost?
Socks a-pair, but where's my mate?
House slippers chomping, it's much too late!

My fridge is home to a curious smell,
Leftovers battle, who'll ring the bell?
Mystery items in tupperware pride,
Last seen in clueless times, they hide!

The vacuum's plotting, it's top secret,
Comfy dust bunnies, just can't reject!
They tumble and dance like they own the floor,
When I sweep, they just ask for more!

On weekends, my couch is my trusty ship,
Navigating snacks with a hunger flip!
Between the potato chips and my sweet tea,
The sofa's where I'm bound to be!

Tarps and Tranquility

In the rain my tarp does sway,
A circus tent, come what may.
Dancing drops on plastic skin,
Laughing at the world within.

Gusts of wind, they play their tune,
Chasing shadows, dodging June.
Waking dreams on puddled floors,
While nature knocks on plastic doors.

Dreams Cradled by Beams

A creaky floor hears bedtime tales,
As monsters march on squeaky trails.
In pajamas, heroes I'll pretend,
With pillows soft, my trusty friends.

Wooden beams above my head,
Guard my secrets, like they said.
When morning comes with real-life tease,
I smile and claim my kingdom, please!

Fortress of Memories

In the attic, treasures lie,
Dusty boxes stacked up high.
With rubber bands and chewed-up pens,
I battle dragons, make amends.

Old photos laugh, their faces bright,
Echoes of our silly fights.
Behind these walls, we've made our mark,
Turning whispers into spark.

Sanctuary of Solitude

Within these walls, I find my peace,
Where wild thoughts can run and cease.
I wear my socks, unmatched, you see,
As comfy as a bumblebee.

The cat gives me a wink and nod,
While I sneeze from dust, oh, God!
With junk food stored in every nook,
I'm the king here, take a look!

Foundations of Belonging

I tripped on my shoes, what a clumsy show,
My house laughs at me, said, "Just take it slow!"
But each tiny stumble steals all my pride,
My silly antics, my loyal guide.

The dog thinks it's funny, he's rolling on the floor,
As I chase my lost socks through the open door.
With walls that see chaos and ceilings that sigh,
I swear this house chuckles when I'm asking why.

Comfort Cradled in Wood

The chair creaks a joke as I settle in tight,
With cushions that whisper, "No need for a fight!"
My snack's made a mess, crumbles by my feet,
But being this silly, oh, it feels so sweet.

The fridge hums a tune as I grab a cold drink,
It knows all my secrets, even what I think.
With shelves full of snacks and laughter on hand,
My home is a circus, oh, isn't it grand?

Echoes of Laughter

The echoes of giggles dance off the walls,
As friends gather 'round for our late-night brawls.
We trip over rugs, we spill all the drinks,
In this funny embrace, it's just what it thinks.

Footprints of chaos mark every room,
Yet in this wild mess, there's never a gloom.
We toast to the memories we've made overnight,
With laughter that sparkles like stars, oh so bright.

Gentle Embrace of a Home

The couch hugs me tight; it knows I won't budge,
While squirrels outside chase dreams, and I just judge.
The walls keep my secrets, they whisper and grin,
In this home where my daydreams and giggles begin.

Every corner's a stage for my crazy charades,
With curtains that flutter, my personal grades.
The broom stands by, ready to sweep up the fun,
In this lively abode, oh, we've only just begun!

Beyond the Doorstep

In slippers I shuffle, a dance with my cat,
The postman arrives and the dog greets with chat.
The neighbors all peer through their curtains with glee,
As I prance like a peacock, just wild and quite free.

The garden's my kingdom, weeds sprout like a crown,
I wave to the world as I tumble right down.
A squirrel steals the show with its antics so bold,
While I ponder my lunch and the treasures I hold.

A Haven from the World

In my fortress of pillows, I giggle and snort,
Remote control wizard, a couch-potato sport.
The fridge is my friend, it never gets cold,
With snacks at the ready, and stories retold.

Oh, the outside looks fine, but there's chaos galore,
I chuckle while hiding, I'm safe from the roar.
So hand me my blanket and cozy my feet,
This castle of comfort is where life's a treat.

The Canvas of My Life

Each room tells a story, a masterpiece made,
With socks as my brushes, and crumbs as the shade.
The ceiling's a canvas where dreams float and play,
As I nap through the hours and lose track of day.

The fridge's a gallery, with sauces proclaimed,
While art from old takeout adorns frames unclaimed.
Behold my creation, it's messy but bright,
As I giggle at life in this colorful plight.

The Resilient Shelter

With curtains a-flutter and snacks piled high,
I fumble through mornings with breakfast awry.
The cat stalks the shadows, the plants wave hello,
While I sip on my coffee, observing the show.

No judgment is passed here, no hurries, no stress,
A sanctuary built from my pajamas impress.
So join in the laughter of this quirky land,
Where the clock runs amok and fun's always planned.

Whims of Weather and Walls

When rain decides to dance and splash,
A puddle forms, oh what a bash!
The roof above, a trusty friend,
Protects me from the weather's blend.

The snowflakes swirl like tiny shouts,
While I'm inside with snacks and doubts.
The storms may roar, the winds may wail,
But inside here, I shall not pale.

The Promise of Protection

With walls around, I'm snug as a bug,
While outside folks might see me chug.
The winds might howl like a hungry beast,
But in this space, I'm at the feast.

A blanket, a snack, and a chair so wide,
A game of hide and seek inside!
The chaos rages with a funny flair,
But here I sit, a cozy bear.

A Cloak Against the Chill

When winter comes with icy hands,
And frost adorns the window strands,
I laugh and snuggle, sip my tea,
Against the chill, I'm wild and free.

The snowman outside, with carrot nose,
Is jealous of my snug repose.
While he stands still, I'm full of cheer,
In this warm haven, I have no fear.

Hearthside Dreams

In front of fire, I hear it crack,
A roaring voice that brings me back.
The marshmallows roast in a giddy dance,
As I recite my silly romance.

The pets all gather, a furry throng,
While I hum to the sizzle and belong.
Against the chill, this joy won't fade,
In this sweet space, I'm overlaid.

Sanctuary of Solace

In my cozy den, cats claim the chairs,
Among scattered socks and my funny affairs.
Pasta for dinner? Oh, that's the plan,
Nothing like noodles to make me a fan.

Duck tape my project? Genius, they say,
My shelves start to wobble, but hey, that's okay!
With laughter and chaos, this life is a game,
It's wild, it's silly, and never too tame.

Secure Within These Four Walls

These walls have seen quips that make spirits soar,
Like my pet goldfish giving me a snore.
A couch that's a trampoline on lazy days,
Where we leap for joy in oh-so-fun ways.

A fridge full of oddities—leftovers galore,
Each bite hides a secret, just what's in store?
In this house of laughter, I wear my crown,
As the king of clumsiness, never a frown.

A Place to Call Home

My hallway's a gallery of shoes in a mess,
Each pair tells a tale, oh, what a success!
With a doorbell that's broken, it sings when it chimes,
Welcoming friends with its whimsical rhymes.

I dance with a mop, oh, what a delight,
Cleaning's a party, so why not invite?
In this structurally questionable, charming domain,
The quirks make it perfect, it gives me no pain.

The Hearth's Gentle Glow

See me flip pancakes with a flourish and grin,
They sizzle and flop, but no way I give in!
With syrup all over, it's a sticky affair,
As I dance in the kitchen without any care.

My dog rolls his eyes at my culinary feats,
While my partner just craves something that's neat.
Yet laughter erupts, as we gather to eat,
In this haven of joy, we make life so sweet.

Guardian of Joy

In a house made of giggles, sprinkled with cheer,
Where socks dance around without any fear.
The fridge plays a tune when it opens wide,
And the cat pulls a prank, oh, what a wild ride!

The chairs have debates on who's the best cook,
While shadows play hide-and-seek with a book.
The laughter flows freely like honey from bees,
With every mishap leaving us weak in the knees!

Nestled in Serenity

In my cozy little nook, where the quirks all bloom,
The teapot sings softly, dispelling the gloom.
Where mismatched curtains dance with delight,
And the clock ticks to the beat of a nightlight!

The couch is a throne for the snuggliest dreams,
With snacks on the table and hot cocoa streams.
The door creaks a tune that makes us all grin,
As laughter bursts out like a pop from within!

Thoughts Beneath the Thatch

Beneath our funny roof, where the stories collide,
The dog tells a tale with a wag and a stride.
Each corner holds secrets, each creak shares a laugh,
Like the moment we found a mouse in the bath!

The ceiling whispers jokes from the nights gone by,
As the windows roll eyes at the clouds in the sky.
With every new mishap, a bond starts to grow,
In the wild, funny chaos – oh, how we glow!

Shelter from the Shadows

In this funny little haven, where time takes a break,
The bed might just argue, for goodness' sake!
With walls made of laughter, and floors that confide,
It's impossible not to wear joy as a guide!

The pantry's a theater, where snacks take the stage,
With popcorn and giggles, we start a new age.
In our merry little fortress, we dance through the spree,
As shadows attempt to join, but they can't find the key!

Whispering Walls

In the corner, a cat snores loud,
While I dream of winning a crowd.
The walls have secrets, they giggle and sway,
As the fridge hums a tune, keeping hunger at bay.

The paint is peeling, it's rather an art,
With every crack, there's a story to start.
My trusty old sofa, a throne for my rear,
It remembers my snacks and every loud cheer.

When the neighbors argue, it's my evening show,
I popcorn my worries, and just sit and glow.
I love this chaos, this quirky ballet,
In the heart of my castle, I snicker and play.

Windows to Warmth

The windows smile, with a gentle beam,
As curtains dance like they're living a dream.
The sunlight spills in, a golden delight,
While dust motes twirl, like fairies in flight.

I tried to clean up, but what a mistake!
Now the broom has a party, for goodness' sake.
The view's quite suspect, but hey, it's alright,
Every glance out reveals a new sight.

My neighbor's dog barks like a trumpet so loud,
While squirrels put on shows, I'm part of the crowd.
These windows are portals to laughter and cheer,
They keep me connected to fun all year.

The Heart's Dwelling

In the kitchen, the spatula sings on the pan,
While the blender's my DJ, making smoothies for fans.
The fridge's a treasure, a land of surprise,
It holds yesterday's pizza, oh my, what a prize!

The couch has held me through thick and through thin,
Endless replays of movies where heroes can win.
With popcorn abundance, the bowls overflow,
In this cheerful fortress, we're never too slow.

My socks go missing, the laundry's a mess,
But this joyful chaos feels more like success.
The heart of this home, it pulses with glee,
In the dance of the daily, there's solace for me.

Bound by Safety

A door that creaks quietly, like a shy friend,
Holds stories of laughter, our joys never end.
Each lock and each hinge guards whims without fear,
In this very shelter, there's love to revere.

When storms start to rattle, I grab my warm drink,
And ponder my mischiefs while the raindrops wink.
My slippers are fuzzy, my blanket a cloud,
In this silly retreat, I'm forever proud.

Beneath this snug ceiling, oh, how we thrive,
With each shared adventure, we dance and we jive.
In the bubble we've built, the world fades away,
With warmth all around, we choose to stay.

Refuge in the Rain

Pitter-patter, droplets dance,
Inside my home, I take a chance.
The leaks are here, the drips a song,
Yet cozy vibes can't steer me wrong.

A towel as my trusty friend,
To catch the streams that seem to bend.
With laughter loud I greet the storm,
In chaos, find my little norm.

The wind may howl, the thunder cheer,
But in my space, I have no fear.
So bring the rain, I'll rock and sway,
In puddles formed, I'll dance and play.

As ducks parade on pools outside,
I'm warm and dry, with jokes as my guide.
This rainy refuge, a quirky spot,
A splashy shelter, a silly plot.

Underneath the Friendly Eaves

The roof above, a playful grin,
With friendly eaves it pulls me in.
I sit and sip my favorite brew,
As drip-drop drips paint skies anew.

Sipping coffee, I spot a gnome,
He shakes his fist; he's far from home.
A mischievous squirrel makes a dash,
But what's a wet day? It's just a splash!

The puddles form a canvas wide,
My thoughts take flight; there's joy inside.
The raindrops play a funny tune,
While I enjoy my rainy boon.

So here I snuggle with my tea,
Beneath the eaves, I'm wild and free.
With chuckles shared and smiles abound,
It's magic found on soggy ground.

Where the Heart Finds Rest

A cozy corner, pillows piled,
In this snug nook, I feel like a child.
With snacks galore, I laugh and play,
Who knew that resting could be this way?

Outside A storm rages with a roar,
Yet I'm content, can't ask for more.
My blanket fort, a silly scheme,
In this blissful chaos, I dream.

The pizza box is now my throne,
As raindrops tap a funny tone.
Every squish, each little dent,
Makes me feel like a royalty sent.

So come, dear friends, and join this mess,
Let's laugh and sing, no need to stress.
In this embrace, where giggles nest,
My heart is full, I've found my rest.

A Nest in the Night

As darkness falls, the stars come out,
In my warm nest, I twist and shout.
The moon peeks in, a cheeky grin,
While I snuggle tight with Port and Gin.

A blanket fort, my fortress grand,
With fairy lights and snacks on hand.
I'm safe from bugs and midnight frights,
This joyful chaos feels just right.

The clock ticks loud, but fears grow small,
As pillow fights and chuckles call.
Under starlit nights, my heart takes flight,
In this hug of fluff, I'm feeling bright.

So let it thunder, let it rain,
In my little dream, there's no such pain.
With laughter ringing through the room,
I'll ride the night, like flowers bloom.

Haven of Warmth

In my cozy nook, the cat takes a nap,
While I brew some coffee, wearing my cap.
The fridge hums a tune, it's quite a hit,
As I dance in my socks, feeling so lit.

The couch is my throne, a cushy delight,
With snacks piled high, I'm ready for night.
Each corner's a treasure, a quirky find,
In this little haven, I leave worries behind.

The Canopy of Dreams

My bed is a cloud, fluffy and round,
With pillows that giggle, oh what a sound!
Each dream that I chase, merry and bright,
In this handmade tent, I stay up all night.

The ceiling fan spins, like a merry-go-round,
While socks throw a party, lost but found.
With a blanket of stars, I cozy and scheme,
Living large in my space, the land of the dream.

Walls that Whisper

These walls have seen laughter, and maybe some tears,
They quip when I'm lonely, they're my favorite peers.
They giggle when I trip, or dance with my broom,
Each paint stroke a story, my heart finds its room.

The windows peek out, with a cheeky grin,
While curtains sway gently, embracing the din.
In this quirky abode, all mischief is blessed,
With whispers of joy, I'll never need rest.

Embracing the Elements

The roof may leak, but it's part of the charm,
With rain drops that rhythm, there's no cause for alarm.
My garden's a jungle, with weeds that are grand,
As I hunt for lost treasures, in this quirky land.

The wind tells me secrets, the doors creak with pride,
As the sun paints my floors, where my wild dreams reside.

A place full of quirks, where oddballs all blend,
In this wacky fortress, I'm my own best friend.

The Fortress of Familiarity

In my fortress, socks are strewn,
And cereal makes for a fine noon.
Old movies on repeat, what a spree,
The fridge hums songs just for me.

Pajamas are the armor I wear,
I keep my snacks without a care.
The pets reign here like tiny kings,
Their tiny paws hold worldy things.

Nesting Amidst the Noise

In a nest of chatter and giggles galore,
I find my peace behind the door.
The laughter echoes, birds take flight,
As I munch popcorn in the twilight.

The vacuum roars like a beastly storm,
While I fashion chaos to norm.
Neighbors' music shakes the walls,
Here I dance, away from calls.

Tranquility Above

Up high on cushions, I take my stand,
While down below, dogs make a band.
My throne is soft, my heart is light,
As I watch the circus unfold tonight.

Overcooked pasta, it looks like art,
In this realm, I play the part.
The world below buzzes like bees,
In my bubble, I sip my teas.

Walls of Kindness

My walls are made of stories told,
Of laughter, mischief, brave and bold.
They listen close to every whim,
In this cozy nook, life's never grim.

Patience hangs on every shelf,
As I attempt to bake, and fail myself.
Yet love spills over, sweet as cake,
In this charming mess, I find my break.

Castles of Comfort

In my domain made of wild dreams,
Cushions like clouds, or so it seems.
Where every snack's a royal feast,
And the cat's the lord, to say the least.

The walls may wobble, but so do I,
We laugh at the past when pancakes fly.
With socks unmatched and shirts askew,
We dance like there's nothing else to do.

The fridge hums a tune of delight,
While I wear a crown that's slightly tight.
Just another day in this curious land,
Where pajamas reign and time is unplanned.

So here's to our castle, slightly askew,
With treasures hidden where memories brew.
And laughter echoes through hall and room,
In our weird little world, there's always bloom.

Echoing Within the Walls

In the echoing halls, secrets glide,
Laughter and snoring both take a ride.
With walls that creak like an old wooden chair,
They tell tales of socks lost without a care.

The kitchen's a battlefield of culinary dreams,
Where cookies once fought and then burst at the seams.
Spatulas wielded like swords in a dance,
Cooking disasters are part of the romance.

Houseplants are yelling, 'Water, please now!'
But I only water them when the cat takes a bow.
Every corner's alive with a quirky delight,
Echoes of laughter fill up the night.

So here's to the walls that listen in glee,
Creating a symphony just for you and me.
No grand architecture, just stories to share,
In this echoing home, love fills the air.

Hidden Treasures of Togetherness

Beneath the sofa, treasures abound,
Lost toys and snacks, that's where they are found.
A treasure map drawn from sheer childish glee,
With X marking spots where crumbs like to be.

We dig through our drawers, a real treasure hunt,
Finding that missing sock, what a good stunt!
There's a sea of oddities, each story a gem,
From mismatched spoons to a forgotten pen.

Tangled up in blankets, we form a mound,
In this ship of snacks, comfort knows no bound.
Board games are battles we boldly proclaim,
And losing just means we'll play the next game.

So let's scrape the surface and look deep within,
For the hidden treasures, where memories begin.
In the chaos we find laughter's sweet sound,
Together we're rich—it's a treasure profound.

The Nest of Nurturing

In the nest where chaos sings the loudest,
Cuddles and snacks make us the proudest.
With crayons and giggles, we build something fine,
A nest of warm moments, pure by design.

Feathers of laughter, all soft and bright,
With stories that shimmer like stars in the night.
The kitchen becomes our whimsical lair,
With cookie dough fights, who's keeping a score there?

Like birds in a tangle, we nestle together,
Grumpy mornings or joyful weather.
With every pillow fort built up so high,
We're queens and kings in our nest, oh my!

So here's to the nurturing, silly and sweet,
With heartbeats as rhythms that won't skip a beat.
In this cozy retreat, doesn't it show?
Our nest is the best when it's filled with love's glow.

Safety in the Everyday

In my abode, I hide away,
Cereal boxes my shields at play.
With socks as plush as clouds above,
I dance through rooms I truly love.

The cat's my guard, the chair's my throne,
In this fortress, I feel at home.
When dishes pile, I fear no doom,
For dust bunnies are my little crew.

If neighbors peek, what fun they'll find,
My yoga mat and slippers twined.
With laughter loud and chaos swift,
I cherish mess in my warm gift.

Beneath the light of cozy glow,
Each silly dance, a funny show.
In ordinary, I find delight,
My silly kingdom, my heart's invite.

The Quiet Whispers of Roofbeams

Once upon a time, in a nook,
The beams above became my book.
They murmured tales of ancient cheer,
While I sipped tea and thought, 'Oh dear!'

I swear they giggled when I tripped,
On scattered toys, the floor I zipped.
The curtain swayed, the shadows played,
I made my peace; let chaos invade.

A sock puppet's my best friend now,
We plot the clean-up of this mess somehow.
As twinkle lights cast sparkly glee,
We jest together, just Sock and Me.

So here's to laughter in my den,
A quirky life, always again.
With beams above that sway in tune,
I feast on fun, my heart in bloom.

Arbored Atmosphere

In my little grove, the world feels light,
Birds chirp songs that tickle my plight.
A blanket fort, my leafy dome,
In here, I've made my silly home.

The coffee pot greets me 'til noon,
With socks that dance like a playful tune.
The chairs have stories, the rugs take naps,
In my wild jungle of cheerful mishaps.

My kitchen's a lab for snacks galore,
Experimenting with treats to explore.
The fridge hums low, then sings a cheer,
While I combine flavors with little fear.

Amidst this arbored joy, I thrived,
In mess and laughter, I'm truly alive.
Each silly moment, I dare to climb,
In this leafy chaos, I find my rhyme.

Canvas of Coziness

On this canvas of pillows and dreams,
I paint my world with giggles and gleams.
With mismatched socks and a cereal bowl,
I find my peace, I find my soul.

The blanket wraps me in fuzzy delight,
As I binge on shows throughout the night.
And in the chaos of crumbs and cheer,
I snicker softly, 'There's no need to fear!'

With open windows that beckon the breeze,
I dance like no one's watching, just me with ease.
Each coffee cup's a trophy of glee,
As I claim victory in my cozy spree.

So here's to the odd, the comfy and true,
To laughter and joy in all that we do.
In this quirky haven, so snug and bright,
I embrace the silly, till morning light.

Pillars of Peace

In my cozy nook, I spin in glee,
The cat takes charge, he's king, you see.
The toast pops up with a resounding cheer,
While I dodge flying socks, never fear!

The fridge hums a tune, a soft serenade,
With leftovers lurking, a pantry parade.
Socks in a pile, my laundry's alive,
In this whimsical chaos, we all thrive.

The couch has become a defensive wall,
Against all that clutter, a brave stalwart call.
With cushions in battle, we hold our ground,
In the realm of comfort, joy does abound.

As laughter erupts, the day's well spent,
With quirky adventures that time truly lent.
Here in my space, life's ticklish race,
Where joy finds refuge, and silliness plays.

The Warmth of Togetherness

Gathered plates stacked high, a feast in sight,
With giggles and jests, we munch with delight.
The dog steals a chip, in sneaky ambush,
While grandma recounts tales of her youth's rush.

Cupcakes on the counter in a frosting spree,
With sprinkles flying fast, it's a vibrant jubilee.
Uncle Joe tells jokes, half-true and absurd,
As we roll our eyes, every punchline heard.

Spoons clanging a tune, a kitchen ballet,
While mom orchestrates chaos, come join the fray.
In the heart of this ruckus, love finds its stride,
With family around me, how can I hide?

Tonight the stars twinkle, we toast with cheer,
For in laughter and warmth, the best moments steer.
Each story a spark, in this bright bonfire,
Where together we flourish, and dreams never tire.

Enclosed in Quietude

In a blanket fortress, I take my stand,
With pillows galore, a soft, cushy land.
The world fades away in a plush embrace,
And my pet hamster gives me a face.

The clock ticks softly, a gentle metronome,
While distant adventures whisper and roam.
Days may rush by with a whirl and a whir,
But here in my bubble, tranquility's stir.

Tea in my cup, a fragrant delight,
As I revel in silence, a blissful respite.
The cat curls up close, like a warm furry thief,
While I tackle the crossword, oh what relief!

The phone is on silent, the world's on pause,
In a moment of stillness, where no one has flaws.
With comic books scattered, and socks on the floor,
In peaceful errand-running, I long for no more.

The Attic of Thoughts

Up in my attic, where memories grow,
Dust bunnies dance in the soft, golden glow.
With boxes of treasures from days long since passed,
I rummage through dreams, some faded, some vast.

A skateboard from high school, my old leather cap,
Among rubber bands and a forgotten map.
I chuckle at photos of hairstyles gone wild,
In the land of nostalgia, I'm forever a child.

Old toys have stories, each action figure, too,
With laughter enshrined, in the attic's debut.
I conjure up battles that never took place,
While the dust moats perform a graceful chase.

It's a haven of whimsy, where daydreams collide,
A space for each thought, where my heart can reside.
In the attic of musings, I wander and roam,
Creating a world that forever feels home.

Bound by Beams of Love

In a house where laughter sings,
A cat plots its mischief schemes.
The fridge hums a secret song,
While the dog snags socks that belong.

Dinner burns, the smoke does rise,
Mom just laughs, she's wise to ties.
Dad's on the couch, snoozing away,
Dreaming of tacos, come what may.

Fuzzy blankets, popcorn spills,
Chasing bugs, fulfilling thrills.
Each room tells tales, smeared with cheer,
Home is chaos, but oh so dear.

Under the roof of chaos bright,
We dance and giggle through the night.
With beams of love, we all align,
In this wacky space, all is fine.

Dusty Corners

Dusty corners hold treasures rare,
Old toys and secrets, what a pair!
Beneath the bed, socks gather dust,
And the vacuum's a monster we trust.

The couch cushions hide coins galore,
And crumbs that once were part of a tour.
Spiders weave webs in playful glee,
In our neglected corner of family.

Last year's birthday balloons float high,
Chasing dust motes as they sigh.
We giggle at what we leave behind,
In this messy abode we've designed.

Who needs a tidy, crisp display?
Our dusty kingdom saves the day.
With love in the air, and chaos too,
These corners spin stories, old and new.

Starlit Skies

Underneath the blanket's embrace,
Nighttime giggles fill the space.
We count the stars, each one a friend,
Finding wishes that never end.

The roof above plays hide-and-seek,
As we share secrets, giggles peak.
Moonlight dances on the floor,
As shadows whisper tales of lore.

We build forts with pillows piled high,
Battling dragons, oh my, oh my!
With laughter echoing through the room,
We chase away any hint of gloom.

A canopy of dreams takes flight,
In our funny little night delight.
Stars twinkle with a knowing grin,
In this haven, we always win.

The Shelter of Memories

In every room, a story brews,
Faded photos, old jokes ensue.
Grandma's quilt finds a cozy spot,
To wrap us in warmth, forget-me-not.

Kids' drawings plastered on the walls,
Scribbled rainbows, and the odd cat sprawls.
We laugh at crayons lost to time,
In this shelter, all things rhyme.

Snacks hidden in a cookie jar,
Counting blessings, oh how far!
With silly dances in the hall,
We find joy in the simplest call.

Memories linger like sweet perfume,
Filling the air of every room.
With love in the mix, we shout, hooray!
In our little chamber, we play all day.

Against the Wind

Battling gusts on a stormy day,
Clothes are flung in a wild ballet.
Umbrellas twist, a comical sight,
As puddles splash with sheer delight.

Yet here inside, snuggled so tight,
We bunker down, avoiding the fright.
Hot cocoa brews, marshmallows swim,
With laughter, the day feels less dim.

Socks mismatched, hair a disaster,
Dancing around, never a master.
We make our own music, silly and loud,
In this jest-filled haven, we're eternally proud.

Against the wind, we stand as one,
In our fortress of fun, there's never a gun.
Just storms outside, but here we stay,
In our cozy spot, we laugh all day.

The Embrace of Everyday Life

In the kitchen, I dance with my tea,
The dog on the floor thinks it's all about me.
Mismatched socks parade, a fashion faux pas,
Living this way has its quirky hoorah!

The fridge hums a tune, a cold serenade,
While leftovers plot their own grand charade.
Toothpaste cap battles, a daily delight,
Under the glow of the overhanging light.

The couch is our throne, where crumbs like to land,
An empire of snacks, it's really quite grand.
With cushions for guards, we rule our domain,
In the castle of chaos, where laughter reigns.

Dishes stack high, a precarious hill,
Each member of the crew has their own special skill.
Yet amidst the clutter, a snug little peek,
Happiness hides in the mess, so unique!

Living with the Lullaby of Rain

Raindrops tap-dance on the window so bright,
A drumming performance, a whimsical sight.
I sip from my mug, cozy blanket in tow,
While puddles outside hold a dance-off in flow.

The roof sings a song, a splish-splash refrain,
As I watch the clouds play their playful game.
My slippers slip-slide across the damp floor,
While dreams of adventures outside linger evermore.

Each drip from the eaves adds to the cheer,
Like nature's own band playing loud and clear.
I imagine each droplet a tickle on nose,
In this giggly contest, anything goes!

When storms come a-knocking, I welcome the sound,
For in my snug bubble, joy can be found.
The world may be wet, but here I still smile,
Humming along with the rain for a while!

The Archway of Embraces

My front door is open, come join the parade,
With shoes by the welcome mat, a curious brigade.
Each greeting a hug, as silly as pie,
I insist on the laughter, no sad faces allowed—why?

Balloons tied to doorknobs, in colors so bright,
An invitation to silliness, morning through night.
The living room's a circus, don't mind the mess,
With juggling of chores, who cares about stress?

We leap over laundry, a maze by design,
High-fives to the couch, where humor aligns.
At every slight stumble, we burst into cheer,
Our halls echo giggles, nothing to fear.

So come take a chance, we'll dodge weird old shoes,
In this doorway of joy, there's so much to use.
With smiles as our entry, the fun starts to rise,
No need for a guestbook to capture the skies!

Secrets Under the Eaves

The attic's a treasure of stories untold,
With dust bunnies spinning their secrets of old.
Old chairs hold meetings of what-has-been-done,
While boxes of laughter sit waiting for fun.

A quilt made of memories, stitched with sweet care,
Each patch tells a tale, a love-light affair.
The spider's their keeper, beneath the lone beam,
Gossiping softly, like whispers in dream.

The creaky floorboards join in with a dance,
With echoes of voices who've taken their chance.
Lost shoes from long ages do tango with grace,
Under eaves, every shadow finds its own space.

So here's to the secrets that dwell in the night,
Where the heart finds its home in soft starlit light.
Under feet and above heads, the laughter extends,
In this hidden haven, where whimsy transcends!

Shadows of Comfort

In my little space, I take a seat,
Cats and socks, a comfy treat.
Dancing shadows on the wall,
Making noise, but it's just the hall.

Lost in thought, I munch on fries,
The ceiling squeaks, it might surprise!
My snack's my throne, so I declare,
In this kingdom, all's laid bare.

The dishes pile, the laundry waits,
The couch, my best friend, celebrates.
A glorious mess, my wild domain,
Each broken toy, a memory's gain.

Beneath this roof, I laugh and skip,
A home-made boat on a friendship trip.
With silly dances, I twirl with glee,
In my fortress stolen from reality.

The Embrace of Overhead

Beneath the beams, my dreams run free,
Where pots and pans form a symphony.
The ceiling hums a joyful tune,
Imitating life's happy swoon.

When rain clouds gather and peasants fret,
My shelter giggles, it's not done yet!
With drippy droplets, a tap dance spree,
As I twirl 'round, the world in glee.

The lamps are winking, their light so bright,
Chasing away the creeping night.
Old walls hug tight, with tales to share,
A comedic saga trapped in air.

With every crack, they hold a joke,
This space of mine, a funny cloak.
The laughter bounces off each wall,
A safe retreat, I risk it all.

Windows to the World

Peeking out, I see a play,
The neighbors dance in bright array.
Behind my glass, I'm queen of sights,
Through windows wide, I claim my rights.

The squirrel's antics send me rolling,
As he steals nuts, it's quite controlling!
I wave at folks with goofy grins,
While hiding snacks—a game that wins!

A dust-smudged pane, my viewing glass,
Each passerby is bound to pass.
Their lives unfold, yet here I stay,
In my daily show, I find a way.

With sunbeams streaking, the curtains dance,
I sprinkle love with every glance.
The windows frame a fabulous scene,
My laughter echoes, happy in between.

Living Beneath the Stars

In my cozy nook, the night invites,
Stars as friends, sharing delights.
The moon waves from a distant place,
As I lounge around in my favorite space.

Tossed on pillows that bounce with ease,
Crashing dreams like a playful breeze.
With snacks galore, I start a feast,
In this wacky world, I'm quite the beast!

Each twinkling light sings out a tune,
Like a serenade under the moon.
With shadows swaying, I laugh aloud,
In this grand space, I feel so proud.

Oh, to be wrapped in starry cheer,
Where every night brings joyful fear.
As the universe spins its strumming song,
I know, in this wild place, I belong.

The Architecture of Affection

In my cozy nook, with socks mismatched,
I laugh at the cat, who's softly attached.
The fridge hums a tune, a sweet serenade,
While I munch on my snacks, in this love parade.

The walls may be crooked, yet they hold me tight,
With echoes of laughter that dance in the night.
I build my own kingdom with chips and some cheese,
In this wobbly palace, I live as I please.

The curtains are mismatched, like colors in art,
But they filter the sun and bring joy to the heart.
Each creak of the floorboards is a friend that I know,
In this odd little space, my happiness grows.

It's not about fancy, it's all in the feel,
With a blanket and smile, my foundation is real.
I dance with my dreams, while the ceiling fans spin,
In this quirky abode, my life can begin.

Wings of Safety

Underneath my ceiling that's ever so bright,
I dream of the sky, take imaginary flight.
The couch is my cloud, soft and fluffy as pie,
With giggles and snacks, as the world drifts by.

No storm can disturb this whimsical nest,
Where socks turn to pillows, and dreams manifest.
The dog thinks he's king, on his throne of old shoes,
While I sip on my tea and enjoy my good news.

The dishes are stacked like a Jenga game high,
But I smile at the chaos, give laughter a try.
In the air, there's a scent of popcorn and glee,
With each silly dance, I'm as happy as can be.

Beneath all the clutter, there's loveliness too,
With every odd trinket, a memory or two.
In this lighthearted haven of whimsy and cheer,
I spread out my wings, knowing safety is near.

Shadows Under the Eaves

In the shade of the roof where the raccoons creep,
I've crafted a haven where secrets run deep.
The sun filters down, like a canvas of fun,
With laughter and play, my day's just begun.

The porch swing squeaks tunes of a whimsical life,
While neighbors quip tales, sans a hint of strife.
Birds gather 'round, singing silly dog songs,
In this joyous domain, where everyone belongs.

Rain dances on shingles with giggles and splashes,
I welcome the storms with warm, cozy flashes.
Each droplet's a note in the symphony high,
As I cozy in blankets beneath the gray sky.

With shadows that dance like the ghosts of my dreams,
Life's more than it seems in these whimsy-filled beams.
Under eaves of affection, I'm forever at play,
In this joyful abode, I'm happily gay.

Foundations of Belonging

Nestled in clutter where socks seem to fly,
I find tiny treasures under the pie.
The floor creaks with stories that tickle my soul,
As I build my adventures in this rock 'n' roll bowl.

Cracks in the plaster appear like old friends,
Whispering tales of beginnings and ends.
The fridge is a palace of leftovers galore,
Each bite holds a memory—who could ask for more?

The ceiling's a canvas, we paint with our laughs,
Each joke is a brushstroke, the heart always drafts.
With silly hat parties and clumsy ballet,
We twirl in this haven, come dance, come play!

The world outside tumbles, in chaos and rush,
Yet here in this haven, there's no need to hush.
With giggles and warmth that forever extend,
In these strong, silly walls, I'm home with my friends.

Where the Heart Finds Peace

In a place that never shakes,
Where squirrels make their little breaks.
The fridge hums tunes I like to hear,
And socks speak secrets with no fear.

A chair that churns with cushions fat,
Got cat hair, but what's wrong with that?
Tangled blankets hug me tight,
As I binge-watch shows all night.

Houseplants nod when I walk by,
Offering shade while I deny.
Dust bunnies dance with a twisty flair,
While I debate my newest hair.

The door's my fortress, the walls my cheer,
No pesky neighbors drawing near.
Here laughter echoes, worries flee,
In this quirky abode, I'm wild and free.

Guardian of My Solitude

A couch that knows too many flaws,
With one spring out, it surely draws.
It guards my snacks like a mighty knight,
Braving crumbs till morning light.

The windows creak with gossiping winds,
While my coffee pot brews ghostly sins.
Draped in blankets, I swirl and play,
In this kingdom, I'll never stray.

The bathroom's my spa, a retreat divine,
Where rubber duckies dance in line.
With candles and bubbles, I'm quite the queen,
In solitude's throne, I reign serene.

Oh poetic escapes of reality's blend,
With pizza crusts and Netflix as friends.
No need for knights in shiny suits,
Just me and my snacks, in cozy roots.

Nestled in Quiet Corners

In a nook where dreams collide,
With cat on lap, I take the ride.
A book's my map to lands so grand,
While laundry piles like shifting sand.

Mismatched socks bring a smile each day,
In this woven mess, I gladly stay.
The corners echo my laughter bold,
Where stories fragrant, silent, unfold.

Mugs hold secrets in chipped designs,
Each sip a laugh, each drip defines.
Caffeine dances, waltzing around,
While my imagination flies unbound.

Cushioned laughter fills the hall,
When shadows play, I heed their call.
In quirky spaces, my heart finds glee,
In this cherished hideaway, it's just me.

Refuge from the Rain

Raindrops tap, a drumline sweet,
While I sip tea, a cozy treat.
Windows fog with stories untold,
Making warriors of the bold.

Puddles outside perform a dance,
Taking chaos, they find romance.
My socks are soaked, but who really cares?
I'm winning the game, while no one stares.

The roof hums soft like a lullaby,
While I think of all the times to fly.
The only storm is the one within,
As I giggle at the mess I'm in.

So here I sit, a pirate proud,
In my fortress, away from the crowd.
With laughter swirling like a wild refrain,
I twirl in joy, my sunshine in rain.

Tales Told in Twilight

In a house made of pillows and a blanket fort,
I host fine feasts of expired popcorn and sport.
Socks for my guests, they're all mismatched,
Clowns in my company, hilariously patched.

The pet cat sits as my kingly advisor,
With snacks in his bowl, oh, what a riser!
He judges my dance moves with a suspicious stare,
I pretend he's the crowd, and I'm the fair share.

Each window's a portal to worlds far away,
Where laundry's a dragon that's ready to play.
Chasing the dust bunnies, my trusty steed,
In this land of make-believe, joy is my creed.

As twilight descends, the laughter won't stop,
My fortress might waver, but I'm on top.
A castle of giggles, it won't end today,
In the heart of my home, where the silliness stays.

Cornerstone of Dreams

My floor's a trampoline, watch out for the bounce,
I trip over shoes, it's a daily announce.
With walls made of wishes and floors of pure charm,
I stumble through life, but it's all part of the calm.

The ceiling's a canvas with clouds of bizarre,
Drawing silly faces, they shine like a star.
A chandelier made of spoons hangs with glee,
My culinary dreams keep spilling the tea.

Here's a chair that squeaks like it's telling a joke,
It creaks in approval, and then starts to poke.
Laughter erupts, like a showbiz affair,
My humble abode is a carnival fair.

In this space where I work out my quirks,
Pants are optional; who needs all the perks?
Each meal is a giggle wrapped tight with a bow,
In my whimsical dwelling, I'm the star of the show.

A Pause from the Chaos

Let's take a moment, let's rest on the floor,
Where snacks multiply like they're keeping score.
With crumbs as my confetti, I call on the cat,
Who's plotting world dominance—where's my baseball bat?

Chaos was knocking, but I shut the door,
With jokes in my pocket, and a heart that won't bore.
The laundry sings ballads of socks on the roam,
While the dishes partake in their own grand tome.

I brew a hot cup of caffeinated cheer,
It reveals that the chaos is just a veneer.
A dance on the table makes all worries freeze,
As laughter erupts with the greatest of ease.

So here's to a life just a tad bit askew,
With spoons in my pockets and laughter anew.
Through the whirlwind of days, may I always find peace,
In a pocket of solace where chuckles increase.

Embracing Solitude

Nestled in silence, my thoughts take a stroll,
In a serene fortress, I find my soul's role.
The couch is my throne, with chips as my crown,
I rule over snacks, the jester is brown.

The fridge hums a tune, a musicy cheer,
While old leftovers bid me a heartfelt hello here.
Tupperware battles—who's left and who's lost?
In my kingdom of solitude, I laugh at the cost.

A quiet retreat with a cup of delight,
My own little universe, all snug and just right.
Here's to cheesy movies and remote control fights,
An ode to my palace on uneventful nights.

With feet up on tables, I embrace every flaw,
Because in this stillness, I'm the star of my saw.
Comic books whisper, tales of the mad,
In my cozy cocoon, I'm delightfully glad.

The Echo of Familiarity

Whenever I sneeze, my neighbors all stare,
They think I'm a goat, not a person with flair.
I dance in the halls, my cat gives a shout,
Living so close, there's no keeping it out.

The fridge has a hum, it sings me a tune,
It winks at the toaster, loves afternoons.
Pants on the line, they wave in delight,
My home is a circus, each day a new sight.

The couch is my throne, where I rule with a game,
Watching reruns, they all look the same.
My dog thinks he's king, with his tail high and proud,
In our charming castle, we're humorously loud.

Under the Gaze of Starlight

Lying in bed, I hear the moon laugh,
It knows all my secrets, good luck with that math.
The stars twinkle brightly, gossiping low,
Do they know I wear socks that don't match? Oh no!

The roof has a leak; it's more of a dance,
When it rains, I grab buckets, I'll take my chance.
Each drip is a beat, a rhythm divine,
Creating sweet music in this home of mine.

My cat thinks the ceiling is a jungle gym,
She leaps and she tumbles—go get it, Slim!
With laughter and chaos, we bask in the night,
Under this cover, everything feels right.

Shelter from the Storm

Thunder shakes windows, but inside I cheer,
It's time for hot cocoa—come grab a chair!
I'll share all my snacks; the popcorn's divine,
Stormy nights like these are just simply fine.

My dog is a pillow, we cuddle and snore,
Dreams of big bones, what could he ask for more?
The wind howls a song, but we're snug as a bug,
Fun in the chaos, all cozy and snug.

Lightning's a strobe light, my living room dance,
With silly moves, we give fun a chance.
So let the rain tumble, we'll laugh through the fright,
In our quirky haven, all feels just right.

Beneath the Safety of the Sky

Clouds are my neighbors, they're fluffy and white,
Hosting tea parties, they float in delight.
I wave from my window, a friendly big grin,
What a nice little world, where I fit in.

The raccoon outside pays nightly visits,
Stealing my snacks—oh, what are his wishes?
I'll leave him some cookies; we'll have a toast,
To the wild life adventures I love the most!

In this little place, where chaos can thrive,
Dancing through days, oh, we're so alive.
With laughter and joy, right here I will stay,
Under the expanse, come what may!

Cuddle of Corners

In my little nook, cats gather round,
On cushions so soft, in laughter we drown.
They knock over mugs, we laugh and we cheer,
In this happy chaos, there's nothing to fear.

Socks on the ceiling, a hat on the chair,
Giant marshmallow that floats in the air.
Walls come alive with our giggles and plays,
In the warmth of the chaos, we spend our days.

A dance with the dust, as the sunlight gleams,
We twirl in our socks, living out pillow dreams.
A fortress of laughter, with echoes of glee,
Who needs a palace when you have a spree?

So here's to the corners, our safe little space,
Filled with fun antics and a warm, cozy embrace.
Laughter our currency, love locked in a bend,
In this cuddle of corners, we never want to end.

Shadows of Solitude

In the quiet hours, a shadow does sneak,
Wandering the hallway, making me freak.
Is it just me? Or a ghost in plaid?
Check under the bed! But don't be too mad.

Silence is golden, they say with a grin,
But the quiet's a trickster, it pulls you right in.
Should I be scared, or should I just dance?
Caught in this limbo, I'm lost in a trance.

I hear the floor creak, like it's telling on me,
Is it a ghost or just old Mr. Lee?
He's lived here forever, and whispers with glee,
"Why worry, dear friend? Just enjoy your cup of tea!"

A flicker of light, or was that a sign?
Perhaps it's just shadows, and they're feeling fine.
I'll laugh with the silence; let's share in the mood,
In the waltz of the shadows, I'll never be lewd.

The Guardian's Gaze

My fridge stands tall, a sentinel bright,
Watching my snacks like a hawk in the night.
With a twinkle of light and a door that creaks,
It guards all my secrets; oh, how it squeaks!

"Eat, drink, be merry!" it whispers with flair,
While I plot my moves like a thief in midair.
Tonight's going big, with popcorn in hand,
As I plot world domination under this brand.

Oh, the guardian fridge, keeper of fate,
Judges my choices, should I; could I? Wait!
With yogurt and veggies all staring at me,
I laugh as I stumble on chips, Oh! Woah, see?

It judges my midnight raids under its light,
But I'm in good company, all snackers unite!
In this funny old dance, I'll munch and I'll graze,
With the cold guardian watching, I'm lost in a haze.

Finding Peace Among the Beams

Cracks in the ceiling, like fingers that wave,
A dance of the beams, oh how they behave!
With each tiny creak, they tease and they echo,
Whispering secrets to squirrels and gecko.

Sunbeams are filters, they pirouette bright,
Painting my world with splashes of light.
A picnic of shadows, on the floor they play,
I'm here in their ballet, come join me, okay?

The beams start to chatter, they giggle aloud,
Sharing warm tales, oh how I'm so proud.
As light streams through windows, weaving its lace,
I find my own rhythm in this cozy space.

So here's to the laughter, the joy in the beams,
In this fun little refuge, I'm lost in my dreams.
With friends of the rafters, I'm truly at ease,
Finding peace in the laughter, a dance with the breeze.

The Embrace of Four Walls

In this cozy space, I roam a lot,
Searching everywhere, but finding forgot.
Socks are on the floor, oh what a sight,
Chasing dust bunnies, I'm in for a fight.

The fridge hums a tune, a sweet serenade,
While leftovers dance, a culinary parade.
A chair is my throne, and the couch my domain,
All hail the queen of the snack-strewn terrain!

Walls whisper secrets, of naps gone too long,
Netflix marathons, who knew they were wrong?
The stamps on my passport are gathering dust,
Adventuring from here, in snacks I trust!

Oh, the doorbell rings, it's a tickle or treat,
Surprise pizza guy, I've got a craving to beat.
Four walls are my comrades, they never complain,
In this fortress of laughter, I'm loony, but sane!

Warmth Within These Walls

Beneath this blanket, I'm snug as a bug,
Coffee's my fuel, in my mug it's a hug.
Pajamas my armor, I fight the day's chill,
Battling laundry mountains, it's all for the thrill!

My cat's got a throne, on my lap he resides,
He's the ruler of warmth, no need for guides.
When the dishes pile high, it's quite a tall tale,
I'll climb that Everest, but first, let me trail!

This space is a haven, where slippers dance free,
With pizza boxes, my stack's quite a spree.
The laughter echoes, it's a joyful din,
As I clutch my remote and let the fun begin!

The oven's a friend, with cookies that sing,
The aroma of chaos is my favorite fling.
I'll host a grand feast, with snacks galore,
In this goofy kingdom, who could ask for more?

Ceiling of Comfort

Look up to the ceiling, what a wondrous view,
They say it's a ceiling, but it's clouds made for two.
I'll count all the cracks, and paint them with dreams,
How many snacks can fit in those seams?

The light flickers on, like a disco delight,
A party for one, on a Friday night.
My pillow reports that the world can wait,
As I navigate life from my blanket estate!

The shelves hold memories, the dust settles deep,
In this cozy retreat, I trade sleep for sleep.
Oh, the daring adventures from this comfy nest,
Building fortresses with cushions, I am truly blessed!

Every thump on the roof, it's just my dance floor,
As my imagination kicks open the door.
I may not leave, but that's perfectly fine,
With my ceiling of comfort, I'm simply divine!

Homeward Bound

I shimmied and shook, from the rain I did flee,
To a place with my snacks, it's just me and my tea.
The doormat greets me, as I stumble inside,
With shoes full of mud, and joy as my guide!

The couch is a comfort, like a hug from the past,
With cushions that whisper, "You're home at last."
In the kitchen, it's chaos, I'm chef and I'm fool,
Gourmet disasters rule this hungry old school!

A maze of my clutter, it's a puzzle for sure,
Each corner a treasure, oh what's that? A drawer!
With half-eaten snacks that make me a chef,
My culinary legacy, just love it to death!

When evening descends, and I plop with a cheer,
The laughter and chaos, it keeps me sincere.
So here's to this haven, where dreams can unwind,
Home is the place where I'm perfectly blind!

Where Solitude Sleeps

In a nook where warmth does creep,
I find my pillow, soft and deep,
With socks that dance, they're quite the pair,
They've claimed the couch without a care.

My fridge fans laughter, it's always there,
With leftovers that seem to stare,
A kingdom of crumbs, a feast for mice,
Who think my snacks are worth the price.

The ceiling holds secrets, surely a knight,
Who battles dust bunnies in the night,
While my slippers plot a great escape,
To party with the cats, oh what a shape!

In this fortress of giggles, chaos, and sighs,
Even the broomstick wears a disguise,
For here I dwell, my kingdom so neat,
Where solitude sleeps, a comfy retreat.

A Canopy of Care

Beneath a sheet that flaps and flails,
I hide from duties, escape my trails,
My blanket fortress, where I take stand,
Against chores and dishes all unplanned.

The ceiling's my friend, it always knows,
When I whisper sweet nothings, how it glows,
While the curtains giggle, swaying in light,
As I dodge reality, holding on tight.

My coffee pot hums a cheerful tune,
Promising java by mid-afternoon,
And all around me, the chaos sings,
In my comfy cocoon, I'm reigning as king!

So here I lounge with snacks piled high,
The world outside can weep and cry,
For in my canopy of care, quite rare,
I find the joy in lounging without a care.

Cornerstone of Comfort

In the corner where cushions collide,
I hunker down, take my silly ride,
With books that tower, a teetering sight,
And popcorn explosions that spark delight.

TV remote, my trusty steed,
Rides me through shows with laughter indeed,
While my cat, the ruler, claims my lap,
As I plot my escape for a glorious nap.

The floor's a jungle of socks and shoes,
A treasure hunt, I never lose,
As I dive into chaos, picking my way,
In this little corner, I joyfully stay.

So here's to the laughter, the spills, the games,
Where comfort reigns and no one blames,
For in each mess, there's a story to see,
At my cornerstone of comfort, just me and me!

Arch of Abode

Under the structure that's slightly askew,
I build my empire, it's just for two,
Me and my snacks, my loyal brigade,
Dancing and prancing in playful parade.

The doorbell rings, but I ignore the sound,
For in this abode, joy's tightly bound,
With pizza boxes that form a throne,
I wave to the world from my plushy zone.

The walls act puzzled, they giggle at me,
As I do the cha-cha in my favorite tee,
While the curtains roll up for a front-row view,
Of my grand display, a sight so true.

So here's to the arch that holds my dreams,
With laughter echoing in joyous themes,
In this quirky palace, I freely roam,
For this little haven, it's happily home.

Safety in Solitude

In the land of clutter I find my peace,
Where socks escape, but worries cease.
Pizza boxes stack like a mini fort,
My couch is my throne, I hold court.

The fridge hums tunes of midnight snacks,
I dance with leftovers, don't cut me slack!
Solo karaoke with a hairbrush mic,
Neighbors applaud when I yell, 'Like!'

In solitude, my quirks shine bright,
I'm the king of chaos, a hilarious sight.
Pajamas my armor against the cold,
In this fortress of mine, I'm brave and bold.

So here's to my kingdom of comfy delight,
With no one to judge, every wrong feels right.
Safety in solitude, oh what a spree,
Just my cat and me, being wild and free!

Under the Shelter of Stars

Lay me down with dreams so bright,
Stars twinkle above, a sparkling sight.
The roof may leak, but who really cares?
I'll just catch raindrops in my spare pairs!

Camping out in my back yard tent,
Amongst stuffed animals, my heart is content.
S'mores in hand, chocolate on my face,
A feast of fun in this starry space.

The dog keeps howling at the moon's glow,
Who's to blame him? It's quite the show!
I join in too; a chorus that's bright,
Under stars, all my worries take flight.

So here's to nights with crickets' song,
The universe hums, and I tag along.
In this cosmic dance, I'm the silly clown,
Under the shelter, I wear my crown!

The Canopy of Companionship

In a house full of jesters, laughter reigns,
Bouncing off walls like joyous trains.
Who needs silence when chaos is bliss?
A friend with a joke is pure happiness!

Tea parties hosted for dolls and bears,
Silly debates over who has the best hair.
We crown the cat, the queen of our crew,
What's better than laughter? Nothing, it's true!

We build blanket forts that reach for the sky,
With snacks hidden where only we spy.
In this tangled web of friendship and glee,
Companionship's treasure is the best key.

So raise your glass of fizzy delight,
To a house full of joy, a whimsical sight.
We may be a mess, but we shine so bright,
In our canopy of laughs, everything's right!

A Warm Embrace of Home

Welcome to my chaos, shoes in a pile,
Where every corner dances with style.
The kettle's singing a sweet melody,
A hug in a cup, oh so heavenly!

Walls echo tales of laughter and fun,
A quirky place where hearts weigh a ton.
Dust bunnies rule while I raise a toast,
To the people I love, who matter the most.

Mismatched socks tell tales of their own,
Each one a story, as uniquely grown.
We've painted our lives in colors so wild,
In this world of mayhem, I'm the happy child.

So come take a seat in this warm embrace,
Forget all your worries, just join the race.
In this quirky kingdom, we'll always belong,
In my heart full of love, we'll sing our song!

Shelter of Serenity

In my cozy nook, the cats take charge,
They claim my lap, it's truly large.
With snacks in hand, I sit and munch,
While they plot world domination for lunch.

The roof above is not just for rain,
It holds my thoughts, my dreams, my brain.
When I see the dust bunnies dance and twirl,
I know that chaos is my kind of whirl.

Neighbors knock, but I'm not home,
I've lost my way in this comfy dome.
In slippers and PJs, I'm a sight unseen,
But in here, I'm a king, like a drowsy machine.

So here's to the walls that whisper and laugh,
In this quirky abode, I'll never take a bath.
With laughter and love, I'll serenade the night,
In my silly sanctuary, all feels just right.

Hearth's Embrace

In the heart of the house, there's a comfy chair,
Where I sit to ponder life, with pitiful hair.
A cup of hot cocoa spills, oh dear,
I guess it's just another reason to cheer!

The fireplace crackles, as my socks do too,
I swear they jump up and dance just for you.
With marshmallows afloat, what a sight to behold,
I'm the marshmallow captain, brave and bold.

Cooking's a challenge in this cozy den,
Last week's rumored stew? It's still in the pen.
But hey, who needs dinner when snacks are around?
I'll feast like a king on each crumb I found!

So let the wind howl and the snowflakes wail,
In this laughter-filled place, I shall prevail.
With friends gathered 'round, we share joyful tales,
In this hearth's embrace, our laughter never fails.

Beneath the Canopy of Dreams

Under a sky of pillows, my fortress stands,
A castle of blankets, woven by hands.
Here in the wild, where the toys roam free,
I am the brave knight, oh can't you see?

With my trusty steed (it's a bouncy ball),
We conquer the room, we'll never fall.
The cats are my guards, with sleepy eyes,
As we plot our escape to some French fries.

My secret hideout has snacks galore,
While the outside world knocks at the door.
The laundry piles high, it's a daring peak,
But my realm of laughter is all that I seek.

So here I shall linger, in pure delight,
Beneath the quilt's stars, I'll sip cocoa tonight.
With whispers of dreams, we'll dance through the gleam,
In this whimsical world, where all's just a dream.

Sanctuary in the Storm

When thunder cracks, it's a party inside,
I'll trade my umbrella for a pillow ride.
The world may be wet, but I stay dry here,
With piles of snacks, I have nothing to fear.

Windows are rattling, and trees may bend,
But in my fortress of laughter, I'll never end.
With socks on my hands, I'm the silly king,
As I dance through the chaos, let the neighbors sing!

Every raindrop a drumbeat, I march to the tune,
As I knit spaghetti by the light of the moon.
Global warming? Please, I can barely boil,
In my zone of comfort, all worries uncoil.

So bring on the storms and the winds that roar,
In this haven of giggles, I'll always want more.
With a heart full of joy and a spirit so free,
This sanctuary whispers, "Just be silly with me!"

www.ingramcontent.com/pod-product-compliance
Lightning Source LLC
Chambersburg PA
CBHW050304120526
44590CB00016B/2477